Famous Places of the World

South America

Helen Bateman and Jayne Denshire

A+

HENRY COUNTY LIBRARY SYSTEM
1001 FLORENCE MCGARITY BLVD.
MCDONOUGH, GA 30252
770-954-2806

This edition first published in 2006 in the United States of America by Smart Apple Media.

Smart Apple Media
2140 Howard Drive West
North Mankato
Minnesota 56003

First published in 2006 by
MACMILLAN EDUCATION AUSTRALIA PTY LTD
627 Chapel Street, South Yarra, Australia 3141

Visit our Web site at www.macmillan.com.au

Associated companies and representatives throughout the world.

Library of Congress Cataloging-in-Publication Data

Bateman, Helen.
   South America / by Helen Bateman and Jayne Denshire.
    p. cm. — (Famous places of the world)
   Includes index.
   ISBN-13: 978-1-58340-801-8 (alk. paper)
   1. South America—Description and travel—Juvenile literature. 2. Historic sites—
   South America—Juvenile literature. I. Denshire, Jayne. II. Title.

   F2208.5.B38 2006
   918—dc22   2006002539

Project management by Limelight Press Pty Ltd
Design by Stan Lamond, Lamond Art & Design
Illustrations by Marjorie Crosby-Fairall
Maps by Lamond Art & Design and Andrew Davies
Map icons by Andrew Davies
Research by Kathy Gerrard
Consultant: Colin Sale BA (Sydney) MSc (London)

Printed in USA

Acknowledgments
The authors and the publisher are grateful to the following for permission to reproduce copyright material:

Cover photograph: Machu Picchu, Peru, courtesy of Photolibrary.com/Timothy O'Keefe.
APL/Chris Lisle p. 14; APL/Ludovic Maisant p. 21 (bottom right); APL/Hubert Stadler p. 15; APL/ Corbis/Joel Creed p. 22; APL/Corbis/Francesc Muntada p. 10; APL/Corbis/Galen Rowell pp. 11, 21 (top left); GettyImages/Tim Laman p. 13 (center right); GettyImages/Samba Photo p. 9; GettyImages/ Maria Stenzel p. 6; GettyImages/Art Wolfe p. 24; iStockphoto/Dan Cooper pp. 4 (center right), 27 (top left); iStockphoto/FabianGuignard p. 4 (center left); iStockphoto/Simon Gurney p. 20; iStockphoto/ Jeff Luckett p. 16 (bottom left); iStockphoto/David Owens p. 4 (left); iStockphoto/Laurent Vetterhoeffer p. 4 (right); Lonely Planet/Krzysztof Dydynski p. 16 (bottom right); Lonely Planet/Paul David Hellander p. 19; Lonely Planet/Eric L. Wheater p. 28; Photolibrary.com/Janqoux Jacques p. 17; Photolibrary.com/C. Marigo Luiz p. 23; Photolibrary.com/Preston Lyon p. 8; Photolibrary.com/Benton Norman p. 25; Photolibrary.com/David Nunuk p. 18; Photolibrary.com/Richard Packwood p. 27 (center right); Colin Sale, Atlas Picture Library pp. 7, 12, 13 (top left), 26, 29.

Contents

When a word in the text is printed in **bold**. You can look up its meaning in the Glossary on page 31.

Wonders of South America

The **continent** of South America consists of five different types of landscape. Its north is covered by dense rain forests. South of the rain forests there are grasslands and desert. The southern tip is **barren** because of the cold. In the west there are mountains. There are many famous places in South America. Some are ancient and some are modern. Some are natural wonders and some have been built by humans.

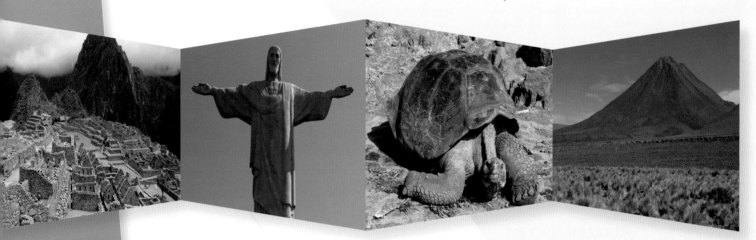

What makes a place famous?

The most common reasons why places become famous are because of their:

- **formation** how they were formed by nature
- **construction** how they were built by humans
- **antiquity** their age, dating back to ancient times
- **size** their height, width, length, volume, or area
- **function** how they work, or what they are used for
- **cultural importance** their value to the customs and society of the country
- **religious importance** their value to the religious beliefs of the country

ZOOM IN
South America has the largest area of tropical rain forest in the world.

Famous places in South America

South America has many famous places. Some are built structures and some are features created by nature.

PANAMA

VENEZUELA

ECUADOR

PERU

Amazon River

Lima

BOLIVIA

BRAZIL

Pacific Ocean

PARAGUAY

Atacama Desert

Rio de Janeiro

CHILE

Atlantic Ocean

ARGENTINA

Patagonia

N
W   E
S

Cape Horn

Key

- Amazon River
- Statue of Christ the Redeemer
- Península Valdés
- Galápagos Islands
- Tiwanaku
- Angel Falls
- Nazca Lines
- Atacama Desert
- Itaipu Dam
- The Andes
- Machu Picchu
- Lake Titicaca

Amazon River

ZOOM IN
The Amazon River is as long as the distance between New York City and Rome.

FACT FINDER

Location northern South America, from Peru to the Atlantic Ocean

Length 4,008 miles (6,450 km)

Width up to 7 miles (11 km) (dry season); up to 25 miles (40 km) (wet season)

Date formed more than 150 million years ago

The Amazon River is a natural feature that is famous for its size. It is the second longest river in the world and it carries more water than any other river on Earth. It flows east from the Andes mountain range to the Atlantic coast. When the river was first formed, it flowed west into the Pacific Ocean. But it was stopped when the Andes rose up in its path. The river changed its course and eventually found its way to the Atlantic Ocean.

▼ The Amazon River acts as a huge drain. It collects the water from the rainfall in South America and takes it to the Atlantic Ocean.

From side to side

The Amazon River crosses almost the entire continent of South America. It supports thriving cities as well as smaller villages. Ships use it to bring products such as clothing, food, and tools to the inland areas. They also use it to take raw materials such as animal skins, Brazil nuts, timber, and rubber out to the coastal areas.

Amazon River basin

The Amazon River is surrounded by the Amazon River **basin**, the world's largest river basin. The basin consists of the largest rain forest in the world and contains over 15,000 streams and rivers. The Amazon River feeds this area and is one of the most famous of Earth's natural wonders.

▲ Some towns along the Amazon River are built over the top of the water. The dwellings are called floating houses.

ZOOM IN

The arowana, one of the 3,000 species of fish in the Amazon River, can leap out of the water to grab beetles from low tree branches.

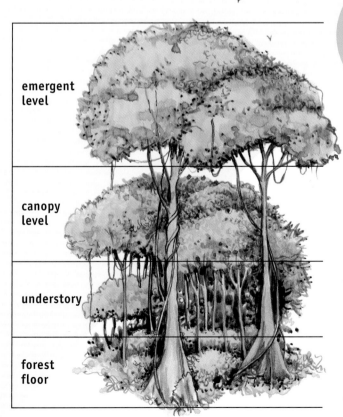

emergent level

canopy level

understory

forest floor

◄ The Amazon rain forest consists of four levels. The emergent level in the tops of the giant trees is the highest. Next is the canopy level, which is in the leafy parts of the trees. Most of the rain forest is made up of the canopy. The understory is under the canopy, and the forest floor is the lowest level of all.

Statue of Christ the Redeemer

FACT FINDER

Location **Rio de Janeiro, Brazil**

Height **98 feet (30 m)**

Weight **1,127 tons (1,145 t)**

Arm span **92 feet (28 m)**

Date built **1926–1931**

The statue of Christ the Redeemer is a built structure that is famous for its size and construction. It is one of the largest statues in the world. It was very difficult to build because of its awkward location. It was extremely difficult to get building materials to the site.

Bits and pieces

The statue of Christ the Redeemer had to be built in a number of separate pieces. French sculptor Paul Landowski carved the head and hands in France. These took him nearly two years to complete. The rest of the statue was constructed by Brazilian engineers Heitor Silva Costa and Pedro Viana.

When all the statue's parts were ready, they were transported by rail to the top of Corcovado Mountain and joined together. In 1931 the statue was finally finished, nine years after planning began. It stands overlooking the city of Rio de Janeiro.

◄ The statue is made from soapstone, which is easy to carve and gives it a smooth surface.

Warm welcome

Christ the Redeemer represents an open-arm welcome to visitors as well as a reminder of Brazil's main religion, Roman Catholicism. There is a chapel for 150 people at its base.

At night, the statue is lit up by floodlights. It can be seen from far inland as well as from many miles out to sea. In the daylight, all of Rio de Janeiro and its bay can be viewed from this world-famous monument.

▲ The statue is exposed to strong winds and sudden changes in temperature because of its position. It has to be cared for to prevent permanent damage.

ZOOM IN
Corcovado Mountain, or "Hunchback Mountain" in English, is named because of the mountain's bent shape, just like a person with a hunched-over back.

Península Valdés

Península Valdés is a natural feature that is famous for its function. It is one of the world's most valuable wildlife areas and is especially important to the **conservation** of the world's **marine mammals**.

Península Valdés is a narrow T-shaped piece of land that juts out into the Atlantic Ocean and forms two sheltered bays with the coastline.

▼ The coastline of Península Valdés
is one of the barest areas on Earth.

► Every August, Magellanic penguins come to the peninsula to nest.

ZOOM IN

Península Valdés is home to so many different types of animals that it has been described as an "open-air zoo."

A safe home

The calmer, warmer waters of these two bays offer protection to many rare **species** of marine birds and mammals, some of which are **endangered**. Elephant seals, Magellanic penguins and sea lions are just some of the marine animals that breed at Península Valdés. This region is one of the largest mating areas of endangered southern right whales in the world.

Land and sea animals

As well as many marine animals, Península Valdés is also home to many species of land animals. These include armadillos, foxes, and sheep, as well as more than 180 species of birds.

The peninsula is the lowest point in South America. One of its lakes is about 131 feet (40 m) below sea level. Its location and its barren landscape help make it a world-famous wildlife conservation area.

INSIDE STORY

Every year at Península Valdés between mid-February and mid-April, sea lions give birth to their pups. This is when killer whales, or orcas, gather to feast on the young sea lions. The orcas patrol the shallow water close to the shore and suddenly throw themselves up onto the beach to grab the young pups. Once they have their meal, they quickly return to the water.

Galápagos Islands

The Galápagos Islands are a natural feature that are famous for their antiquity and their unusual animal life. For millions of years, these volcanic islands have been separated a long way away from any other land. Because of this, there are animals and plants now living on the Galápagos Islands that do not exist anywhere else in the world.

ZOOM IN
Some land iguanas in the Galápagos Islands grew webbing between their claws and became marine iguanas.

▼ Most of the Galápagos Islands are very rocky with only low shrubs. In some higher areas there are patches of moss, ferns, and forests.

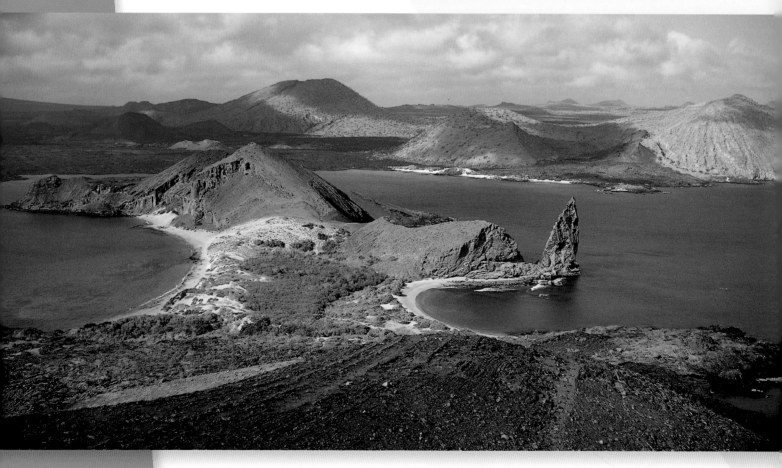

◄ One species of land iguana lives only in the Galápagos Islands.

▼ The giant tortoise of the Galápagos Islands is thought to have the longest life span of any animal on Earth. It can live up to 150 years.

A long journey

Some people believe that to get to the islands, the birds must have flown from Central and South America, and that the land animals must have floated across the sea on pieces of **driftwood**. The plants were probably carried there as seeds by the birds.

Fitting in

It is thought that the animals and plants **evolved** to fit in to their new **environment** once they settled on the islands. For example, the Galápagos cormorant, a seabird, does not grow proper wings anymore because it does not need them. It is not hunted by any animal on the islands, so it does not have to try to fly away from anything. It is the uniqueness and strangeness of the animal life of the Galápagos Islands that make these islands famous around the world.

Tiwanaku

ZOOM IN
Five different cities have been excavated at Tiwanaku, one built on top of the other.

FACT FINDER

Location southern shore of Lake Titicaca, Bolivia

Date built 100–1000 A.D.

Size 2 square miles (6 sq km)

WORLD HERITAGE SITE since 2000

Tiwanaku is a collection of built structures that are famous for their antiquity and their religious and cultural importance. It is thought that this ancient city began as a small village about 100 A.D. By about 500–750 A.D. Tiwanaku was a flourishing city, a cultural and religious centre in South America. By about 1000 A.D., however, it had begun to collapse, possibly because the lack of water from severe droughts affected agricultural production.

▼ Kalassaya is the main temple of the city. It is believed to have been dedicated to the sun. It was used to observe the movement of planets and stars in the skies.

Advanced architecture

The temples, pyramids, walls, and courtyards of Tiwanaku are examples of quite advanced architecture. They are made up of carved stone blocks fitted precisely together. It is believed that the city was surrounded by a **moat**.

How people lived

From the ruins of the city, **archeologists** can piece together how the people of Tiwanaku lived. Their temples and monuments show that they were strongly religious. The people had developed an agricultural system of raised beds for planting crops that were watered by small **canals**. It is estimated that between 20,000 and 40,000 people lived in and around this famous ancient city.

ZOOM IN
Some of the large stones used in the building of the city weighed up to 98 tons (100 t).

▲ The Gateway of the Sun was cut from one block of stone. It was used as a solar calendar.

► Artists try to guess how the city of Tiwanaku used to look when people lived there. They use the ruins as a guide.

Pyramid of Akapana

Gateway of the Sun

Kalassaya Temple

Sunken Courtyard

Angel Falls

FACT FINDER

Location southeastern Venezuela

Height up to 3,212 feet (979 m)

Width 351 feet (107 m)

Date formed more than 2,500,000 years ago

Angel Falls is a natural feature that is famous for its size and beauty. It is the tallest waterfall in the world, dropping from a height of over almost 3,200 feet (1,000 m). The water from Angel Falls drops such a long way that people cannot see all of it at once unless they fly over it. It is 19 times taller than the Niagara Falls in the United States.

ZOOM IN
The local name for the falls is "Devil's Mouth."

Origin of the falls

No-one really knows exactly where the water first collects. The heavy tropical rain fall is trapped by a series of cracks and **gorges** at the top of the **plateau** called Devil Mountain. The water shoots out from its extraordinary height down a sheer cliff and eventually drains into the river below.

◄ The water from the falls flows into the Churún River.

► It used to be almost impossible to get close enough to see Angel Falls, but these days, people can get there by canoe.

Mist covered

The top of Devil Mountain is often covered in a mist. In the rainy, or wet, season (from June to December), Angel Falls sometimes splits into three separate sections.

Behind the waterfall is an immense natural cave. The water collects in a huge pool in the tropical jungle beneath the falls. In the dry season (from January to May), however, this world-famous waterfall sometimes fades to nothing more than a thin stream of water.

▲ Angel Falls begins about 50 feet (15 m) from the top of Devil Mountain.

Nazca Lines

FACT FINDER

Location 186 miles (300 km) south of Lima, Peru

Size 193 square miles (500 sq km)

Date drawn 2,000 years ago

WORLD HERITAGE SITE since 1994

The Nazca Lines are a feature formed by humans. They are **geoglyphs**, or drawings on the ground, that are famous for their antiquity. They were made by the Nazca Indians who lived in the Nazca Desert region between 300 B.C. and 800 A.D.

All shapes and sizes

The drawings are large patterns composed of shapes, straight lines, and figures of animals. They were made by scraping away the desert's dark red rocks, leaving grooves of lighter soil showing underneath.

There are more than 300 drawings, none of which is repeated. Each picture is drawn using a single, unbroken line.

It is believed that these figures were first drawn on a small scale and then expanded onto the landscape by means of a simple **grid**.

◄ The Nazca Lines are difficult to see from ground level, but are plainly visible from the air.

► Drawings such as the "Spaceman" can be seen from the air. They are preserved by the desert's dry climate and by winds that blow the sand out of their grooves.

ZOOM IN
The lines remain straight even when going over hills and other rough country.

A variety of animals

The animal drawings include a monkey, a whale, a spider, a fox, a lizard, and several birds. The monkey measures 328 feet (100 m) and the lizard is 591 feet (180 m) long.

The origin and purpose of the famous Nazca Lines are still a mystery. No one can explain why the Nazca Indians drew patterns and pictures that can only be properly seen from the air.

INSIDE STORY

There are many theories on why the Nazca Lines were constructed. Some people think that they are linked with astronomy and point to the position of the stars and planets. Others believe the animal patterns are pictures of gods and spirits, and that the site is an outdoor temple. Still others believe that because the lines are only visible from the air, ancient astronauts built the lines as a landing field for some sort of spacecraft.

Atacama Desert

▼ The Atacama Desert has many salt basins, such as this one in Bolivia. Salt basins were once lakes that became salty, then dried up, leaving only salt behind.

The Atacama Desert is a natural feature that is famous for its climate and its function. It is the driest place in the world. It is also the world's only source of natural sodium nitrate, which is used to make gunpowder and agricultural fertilizers.

A varied landscape

The Atacama Desert is made up of salt basins, **lava flows**, and sand. It is cooler than most other deserts. It rains only once or twice every 100 years, and in some areas, rain has never been recorded.

In the Atacama Desert there is often fog, but no rain. Most of the moisture comes from the mist that rises from the Pacific Ocean. Higher up, where the desert extends into the Andes, the moisture creates snow rather than rain.

◄ Small communities in the valleys are able to raise farm animals and grow crops. They use water that flows in streams from the snowy mountains.

ZOOM IN

Because the Atacama Desert is so dry, the bodies of buried Native Americans have dried perfectly and been preserved into mummies.

▼ Small patches of snow remain on the mountain tops. Sometimes it melts to form small rivers.

A hard life

Some plants and animals have **adapted** to the harsh environment. They are able to survive by depending on the combined moisture from fog and dew.

Humans have lived in the famous Atacama Desert for many thousands of years. **Mummies** have been found that date to 9,000 years ago. These are some of the oldest mummies so far found on Earth.

Itaipu Dam

ZOOM IN

In the local language, the name "Itaipu" means "singing stones."

FACT FINDER

Location On the border of Brazil and Paraguay

Height 643 feet (196 m)

Width 4.8 miles (7.76 km) from bank to bank

Date built 1975–1982 (main dam)

Itaipu Dam is a built structure that is famous for its function. Built across the Parana River, it is the world's biggest producer of **hydroelectricity**. It supplies electricity for all of Paraguay and most of southern Brazil.

Water problems

Itaipu Dam was built to ease the water shortage problems brought on by droughts. Engineers had to move the course of the Parana River, which is the seventh largest river in the world, around the construction site. It took almost three years for workers to make another channel for the river to use while the dam was being constructed.

▼ Itaipu Dam consists of a series of concrete dams as well as spillways, or overflows. These control the amount of water allowed to pass.

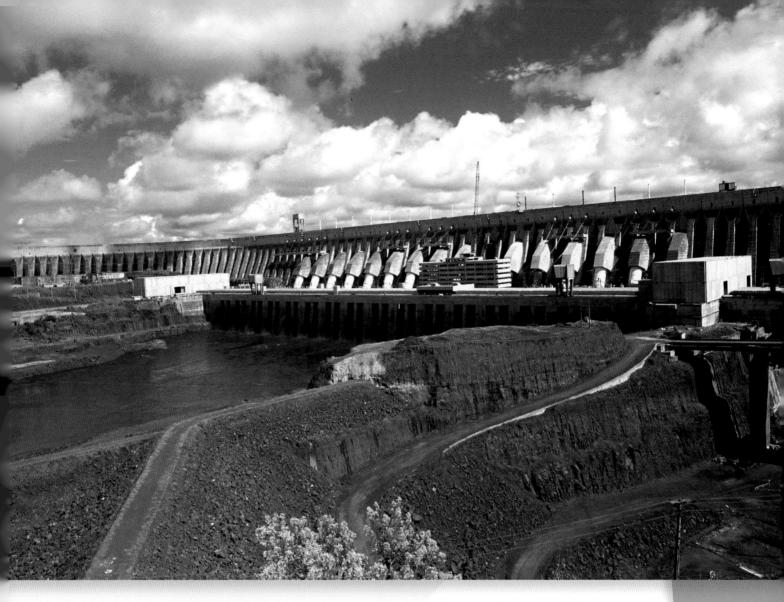

▲ The amount of concrete used to build the dam would be enough to build 15 channel tunnels between France and England.

Power station

The power station at the Itaipu Dam has 20 **generators** that are the largest in the world. An artificial lake was created behind the dam by flooding the land, which was mostly rain forest. Before the flooding, **fossils** that were 8,000 years old were saved. Thousands of animals were caught and released in new nature reserves. The governments of Brazil and Paraguay created these new wildlife areas and replanted the forests. They wanted to make sure that the animals and plants would be protected from the construction of this world-famous dam.

ZOOM IN
It took 30,000 people seven years to build Itaipu Dam.

The Andes

FACT FINDER

Location west coast from Panama to Cape Horn

Length 5,530 miles (8,900 km)

Width up to 500 miles (800 km)

Date formed over the last 65 million years

The Andes mountains are natural landforms that are famous for their size. They are the longest mountain range in the world. The Andes stretch from Panama in the far north of South America to Cape Horn at its most southern tip.

The Andes contain many volcanoes, some of which are still **active**. They also make up one of the highest mountain ranges in the world.

▼ The Andes form a natural boundary between Chile and Argentina.

24

Recent formation

The Andes are one of the most recently formed mountain ranges on Earth. They were formed by the movement of the Earth's surface. When parts of Earth's **crust** are pushed together hard enough, the middle part is forced up into a hump that becomes a mountain range.

Different climates

The Andes can be separated into three distinct climates. The northern Andes are hotter and wetter. The central Andes form the widest part of the mountain system where the weather is milder. The southern Andes are in the very southern tip of South America and so are much colder. The famous Mount Aconcagua, the highest mountain in South America, and Ojos del Salado, the world's highest active volcano, are both in the southern Andes.

▲ Mount Aconcagua, which is an extinct volcano, is the highest mountain in the Andes.

ZOOM IN

Ecuador, in the northern Andes, has more volcanoes than most countries in the world. It has over 30 volcanoes, and eight of these are considered active.

Machu Picchu

FACT FINDER

Location **Peru**

Size **2 hectares (4.9 ac)**

Date built **1450–1500**

WORLD HERITAGE SITE
since 1983

Machu Picchu is a collection of built structures that are famous for their construction, antiquity, and their religious and cultural importance. This city was built by the Incan people high in the Andes mountains in Peru. The Incas began as a small tribe in about 1200 and grew to a mighty civilization by about 1400.

▼ The ruins of Machu Picchu have helped historians piece together the details of how the Incas lived.

ZOOM IN

As fall came to Machu Picchu, an Incan priest held a ceremony to "tie" the sun to a special sundial. The Incas believed this ceremony might stop the summer from leaving.

▼ The terraces were used as flat areas for building houses in rows, and for growing crops.

▲ Historians believe that the houses used to have thatched roofs, such as the one added here.

Well preserved

The site of Machu Picchu is almost undamaged. The ruins consist of palaces, baths, temples, storage rooms, and about 150 houses. Although Incas had no iron tools, they carved huge stone blocks from the mountain and made them fit together perfectly without using **mortar**.

An ancient fort?

Some people believe Machu Picchu was built as a fortress against Spanish invaders, and some believe it was a ceremonial or religious site. Others believe it was a palace or a holiday place for the Incan royal family.

The houses in this world-famous city were surrounded by drainage channels and **terraces**. The terraces were filled with soil that they used to prevent **erosion** and mudslides, as well as to grow their crops.

INSIDE STORY

In 1911, the ruins of Machu Picchu were discovered by an American explorer, Hiram Bingham. He was looking for the ruins of where the Incas last fought off the Spanish invaders, when an old Native American man offered to guide him to some hidden ruins. They climbed a steep path through the forest. As they got higher, Bingham could see traces of terraced fields, when suddenly a maze of ruined walls appeared. It was the site of Machu Picchu, which had never been found by the Spanish invaders.

Lake Titicaca

Lake Titicaca is a natural feature that is famous for its size. It is South America's largest freshwater lake and the highest lake that large vessels can sail on in the world. It is fed mainly by water from rivers formed by the melting snow of the Andes. The water level in the lake can vary by as much as 16 feet (5 m) through the year.

▼ Lake Titicaca is surrounded by the high peaks of the Andes.

Many islands

There are more than 40 islands in Lake Titicaca. Some of these have ruins of Indian civilizations that existed many hundreds of years ago. On the southern shore of the lake, archeologists have found the ruins of Tiwanaku, one of South America's first civilizations. Even below the surface of the lake, archeologists have discovered a temple believed to be at least 1,000 years old.

Traditional lifestyle

The Aymara people, who live by the lake, still live in much the same way as their **ancestors** lived. They fish the rainbow trout in the lake, some of which are 3 feet (1 m) long.

Lake Titicaca is also famous for the islands of Uros, which are made out of reeds and float on the lake. The local people make their homes and their furniture out of the reeds.

ZOOM IN
The frog *Telmatobius culeus*, which can grow up to 30 centimeters, lives in the lake and almost never surfaces.

ZOOM IN
Lake Titicaca is so high that visitors suffer from breathlessness and faster heart beats because of the lack of oxygen.

▲ The Uru and other lake dwellers make boats by tying together huge bundles of totora reeds that grow around the lake.

Famous places of South America

Our world has a rich collection of famous places. Some are spectacular natural wonders and some are engineering or architectural masterpieces. These famous places in South America are outstanding in many different ways.

Wonders formed by nature

PLACE	FAMOUS FOR
Amazon River	The second longest river in the world Carries more water than any other river in the world
Península Valdés	One of the most successful protected marine wildlife areas in the world
Galápagos Islands	Home to many unique species of plants and animals One of the most active volcanic areas in the world
Angel Falls	The highest waterfall in the world
Atacama Desert	The driest place in the world
The Andes	The longest mountain range in the world One of the highest mountain ranges in the world
Lake Titicaca	The highest lake that large vessels can sail on in the world

Masterpieces built by humans

PLACE	FAMOUS FOR
Statue of Christ the Redeemer	One of the largest statues in the world built on one of the most difficult construction sites in the world
Tiwanaku	An important religious and cultural center in the southern Andes before the Incan civilization
Nazca Lines	The best known geoglyphs, or pictures drawn in the ground, in the world
Itaipu Dam	The largest producer of hydroelectricity in the world
Machu Picchu	One of the few ancient Incan cities whose buildings have survived to modern times

Glossary

active able to erupt at any time

adapted changed to adjust to new conditions

ancestors relatives who lived a long time ago

archeologists people who study the people and customs of ancient times from the buildings they left behind

barren not able to grow plants

basin a large hollowed area in Earth's surface

canals artificial waterways for ships which can also provide water to farms

conservation the protection of animals and plants

continent one of the main land masses of the world

crust the hard outer surface of Earth

driftwood wood that is floating on water or has been washed ashore

endangered in danger or at risk

environment all the features of an area, such as trees, land, and water

erosion the breaking down and wearing away by the elements of the weather, such as water, wind, and ice

evolved developed gradually to become something else

fossils the remains of plants or animals from long ago, preserved in some way

generators machines for producing electricity

geoglyphs lines drawn in the earth

gorges narrow valleys with steep, rocky walls on both sides of a river or stream

grid a pattern of evenly spaced squares

hydroelectricity electricity produced using falling water as a source of power

lava flows streams of the hot liquid rock that comes out of a volcano

marine mammals sea animals whose young feed on their mother's milk

moat a deep, wide ditch, usually filled with water, surrounding a town to help keep invaders out

mortar a mixture used for joining bricks together

mummies dead bodies that have been specially treated to stop them from decaying

plateau a large flat area of high ground

species a group of animals or plants that can reproduce their own kind

terraces sloping land that has been made into flat areas like steps

Index